Rise to Freedom

Her Story in Rhyme

VANESSA B SMITH

BALBOA.
PRESS

A DIVISION OF HAY HOUSE

Balboa Press books may be ordered through booksellers or by contacting:

Balboa Press
A Division of Hay House
1663 Liberty Drive
Bloomington, IN 47403
www.balboapress.com
1 (877) 407-4847

Because of the dynamic nature of the Internet, any web addresses or
links contained in this book may have changed since publication and
may no longer be valid. The views expressed in this work are solely those
of the author and do not necessarily reflect the views of the publisher,
and the publisher hereby disclaims any responsibility for them.

The author of this book does not dispense medical advice or prescribe the use
of any technique as a form of treatment for physical, emotional, or medical
problems without the advice of a physician, either directly or indirectly. The
intent of the author is only to offer information of a general nature to help
you in your quest for emotional and spiritual well-being. In the event you use
any of the information in this book for yourself, which is your constitutional
right, the author and the publisher assume no responsibility for your actions.

Any people depicted in stock imagery provided by Getty Images are
models, and such images are being used for illustrative purposes only.
Certain stock imagery © Getty Images.

Print information available on the last page.

ISBN: 978-1-9822-1866-9 (sc)
ISBN: 978-1-9822-1867-6 (e)

Balboa Press rev. date: 02/07/2019

Dedication

For my sons Jabari and Ta'ziyah Ngozi.
Follow your bliss.

Acknowledgement

To my Mum and Dad, Sarah and Nevil Smith. You laid the first foundation.

To Kondwani Ngozi who has stood beside me, behind me and in front of me in the best and the worst of time.

To my brothers Clive Smith who encouraged me to keep going and Winston Smith who shared my writing among friends.

Healers are spiritual warriors who have found the courage to defeat the darkness of their souls, awakening and rising from the depths of their deepest fears, like a Phoenix rising from the ashes. Reborn with a wisdom and strength that creates a light that shines bright enough to help, encourage, and inspire others out of their own darkness.

Contents

Price Of Love

Life is for living

Culture

Peace

Anticipation

Elation
Contained
Within
Whilst daily
Creating
Bringing
into being
Ideas
Now
Taking shape
Filling
out.
Breathing
Life
Into
Thoughts
Of my making
Exciting
Patiently
Waiting
For the day
Of unveiling
A dream

That became
A reality
Through
Acting
On
Gut feeling!

Burn

Smothered
Beneath the weight
Of the self-limiting bushel.
Puffs of smoke
Her attempts
To survive the dust and the rubble
But ah. It is time!
She senses the change in the wind
A crackle, a sparkle,
Reignited is her flame.
This girl is on fire!
Ablaze!
And her true magnificence, reclaimed.
My darling, Burn!
Now you remember your name,
The one with which you first came.
Melt the hearts and souls
Of those who have become hardened.
Those who too have forgotten
The art of living,
Confined to the mundane,
Lost the will for change.
Burn!

Burn intensely!
Rekindle their desire
To once again emerge and discover
Just like you
The beauty of their own fire!

Seekers of Wealth

World changing
So amazing
As mind clears
And hearts open
Deeper, wider through meditation
Nothing in the material world compares
To the treasures uncovered here
Illusions lay bare.

Priceless gems
Peace, joy, compassion and love
They very essence of who I am
Carry me daily
Successfully connect me
To kindred spirits
Who too take the time
To seek diamonds and nuggets of gold within
Internally, excavating.

Wealth, strength and power
Is not always loud
Bold yet so subtle each one is
Shining brightly through the titles in a crowd

It recognises
That to all honour is due
Speaks words of wisdom to inspire
Never to subdue.

The quest is to continue spiralling inwards
Where wealth in abundance resides.
To those who are open, thankful
And live with a heart of gratitude,
The priceless outpouring
Governed by Universal law and Order,
Cannot be denied.

All that glitter is not gold
If you have not yet come to know it
Then here you have been told.
There is a beam of light that shines within
That the dazzling photons without
Can sometimes cause to appear dim
But you shall know the truth
And the truth will set you free.
Just dare to be still, completely
And from a viewpoint, which sits mid brow
Awake and the greatest wealth will be revealed in the now.

Your World and Mine

I accept that you will never see my truth
Yours is ingrained
And like a runaway train
Life rushes by
And the beauties here to you
Become just flashes of colour.
To me
You miss the splendour
The details
The outline
The smells
The texture.

Focused purely on the destination
No found joy in the physical creation
Because this world is not your home
You are only passing through
Your treasures await you
Somewhere beyond the blue.

I totally get it
The fearful reaction
Plucking a verse

To correct my right
That is perceived to be so wrong
But no longer am I afraid
To enjoy the fruits from the tree of life
Of which the serpent offered
A life fulfilling choice to be wise.
The shedding of the old
That did keep me safe
I know now
Could never lead to my eternal demise
So I allow Kundalini to stir and rise.

I am standing on firm foundation
I am flowing with creativity
I am growing in personal power
I am love and full of compassion
I am hearing and speaking my truth
I am seeing mysteries unfold
I am connected to the Supreme Life Force

I am in the Father and the Father is in me
I am the way the truth and the light
I am come to have life
And to have it more abundantly
That's my story.
When I look in the mirror
Who do I see?
I am that I am
Embracing all the goodness of life
As who else
But Me!

Where I am meant to be

A little fuller in body and face
As most of us are now at our age
She walked into the store
I could not ignore
Slight frustration
As I struggled for a few seconds
Trying to remember her name
I called out just the same
And off my tongue, there it came
She turned
With delight
And we shared an embrace

A moment of her lunch time
To stop and rewind
Then to fast forward to where are now.
Such different lives
That could have been almost identical
33 years she in her 9 to 5
With the same company
There were two roles

And she and I were both successful
Half way through
Our City & Guilds
Teacher insisted
We were the right candidates to apply.
Accepted,
Her parents agreed
Mine denied
me the opportunity
Go back to 6th form
The secretarial course
I had to complete
Qualification to them more important
Than of me, at that time, earning my keep.

For the rest of my day
Fleeting thoughts became
Brush strokes
Painting beautiful pictures
Of what my life could have been
The colour palate
An abundance of green
As a result of
Job satisfaction and financial security.

My life has been convoluted
Meandering in ways never imagined
Knowledge of life and self-love
Have been my Degree and Masters

And now that the most important questions
About how to live an authentic life
Have all been answered
I am now ready
To enjoy the fruits of my labour.

Out in the cold

Into place things have fallen
Now I see clearly the life that was chosen
What did unfold
Kept her out in the cold.
She could feel the love was tainted
For not becoming
All that he had wanted.

Grown and out in the world
She was a daddy less girl
And what continued to unfold
Kept her out in the cold
The energy of being a disappointment
Unconsciously governed her choices
In her pursuit of being loved
Made her search in questionable but necessary places

The realisation overwhelmed
That until she could truly love herself
All that would unfold
Would keep her out in the cold
From people pleasing time to disconnect
and herself respect

By tapping the power within
external approval
no longer attempting to win.

Forgive him and herself a must
And her truth she now trusts
What has come to unfold
She is no longer out in the cold
With the lessons now grasped
And used wisely
The warmth that radiates from her heart
Allows her, in her truth to stand boldly

Our trials do come to break us open
To reveal within us is heaven
With the truth that unfolds
We can choose to come out of the cold.

In the
Beginning.

Expectations

A glimpse of your gift
You recognised when just aged 5
In your first creation there you stood
Feeling so alive.
Peers and teacher the crowd
You took your first bow
There your God-given talent
Came under the spot-light.

He said be number one
And to no-one bow
If you don't know,
I will show you how
I'll stand by you
I will defend you
All that man wants,
Is for you to do as he says
Make him feel proud.

Hold up your head,
And try to do better
Get a profession
You must lift yourself higher

Be a lawyer a doctor
A scientist a teacher
Try to be somebody,
Don't want you to come like me
And suffer.

In a young fertile mind
The seeds were sown and planted
It was necessary to be
Exactly what they wanted.
Expectations the weed
That infiltrated the need
To live from your heart
As the Creator intended

On life's treadmill
You took the strides of expectation
Doing your best to acquire
The high profile profession
Determined and focused
Success was a must
But deep in your heart
You knew not your true direction

All came to a halt,
Time to stop spinning the wheel
Just to make others happy,
This was no longer a deal
It was time to reconnect
Not to forget
We only live once

Can't allow our fate
By others to be sealed.

Prayer and meditation
Became the way back home
Was such a joy to spend
Precious time alone.
Seeking uncovering
The unique blessing
That which you caught a glimpse of
So many years ago.

Was not easy to deal
With the anger and accusations
That came with the knowledge
You stepped out of mainstream education
A new understanding
Outside popular thinking
Was absolutely necessary
For my soul's liberation.

Happy you are and it is now time
To share with the world
Yourself, the Devine
Words of wisdom
That through you come
From the journey of removing
To you, all that never belonged.

The Journey

A shift,
Lift,
Head held high,
I can no longer deny
All that I am
Powerful and strong,
Enough and more
This is the score
Now etched in every cell of my body
Consciously being guided by the script of my soul
I now can live my true story.

It must be,
That we,
Start this journey
Bound, in order to set ourselves free
We meander our way
Through experience after experience
Learning how to become less resistant
Until we remember
Who we are
Finally.

For the most part, trying
Trying to understand
Our place in this world.
Although I do not say it
Instead I play it out
When subconsciously
I recognise
My features and complexion differ greatly
From the boy or girl
That makes up the majority in my small world.

Stockings on my head
Long hair,
Burns to my ears and scalp
Straight hair,
Techniques that mum insist will give me
Narrow nose,
And why do the dark skinned children in the school play
Never get the leading roles?

I grow up believing
That I was just
A second class citizen.
Aged 10, puppy love.
Who I saw
As my first boyfriend
Brought home the reality
That I could see
All around me.
Skin too black he told me,
Hair to short and kinky

And so chose my long haired white best friend.

What I could not change was my skin
But now grown,
You would never see me without my head coverings
Curly perms and straighteners
Removed the pepper grains
And moving with the trends
Add ons,
Plaits and weaves
Gave me
A sense of equality.

I remember when I first decided
I would go natural.
Dressed to the nines
I stood in line
Waiting to enter the dance.
From a brother
Disgusted looks and stares
The mocking sneaky glance,
At me in my natural state.
Self-confidence, still yet
Not strong enough,
To go back to strutting my stuff
Confidently in the fake
I just could not wait.

I suppose my parent's faith in religion
Did not help my situation
Taught me that

I was born in sin
Now added to the equation.
I had to accept
A white God whose son died to set me free
The same God
Used to enslave
My ancestors
Was now here to wash me
As white as snow
And from hell's damnation,
He would deliver me.

It was there
Right there in the Bible
Something grabbed my attention
In all the centuries and years
That others had been reading
As clear as clear can be
It was no big revelation
Had they not connected
Afrika was the cradle of civilisation?
That could only mean one thing to me
If I'm created in Gods image
Then must I not
As a child of God
Be imbued with the same power as He
And He not be
As black as me?

African culture and spirituality
Seeking and I was searching

Groups left me disillusioned
Shoulds and shouldn'ts
And so many contradictions
And so my journey continued
And Buddhism called me by name.
Coming closer to the truth
That all power lies within
With single minded thought
I could manifest
My heart's desire
Channelled through consistent
Nam yo renge kyo chanting.

Having learned what I needed to learn
It was time to make the next move
Family issues
Now to contend with
My new understandings
Choice of living
I was drilled to prove.
No sense
None of this meant to them
I was just straight plain crazy
Too far removed
From what we were raised to believe
I became the conversation of mockery.

Forced out like Joseph
Beaten and bruised
Fight back I could do no more
A life of loneliness

Disconnection
Pain
And deep dark depression
Unlike anything I had experienced before.
Solitude
I went through
This story I had to shake this
I had to break this
15 years a victim in the making
I was stuck
And as far as I could tell
The only one that was hurting.

Sometime later
I wrote to Iyanla
And believe you me,
3 weeks later
I sensed the weight
I had been bowed under
Lift and I felt a sense of ease.
The final acceptance and forgiveness came
When a dear one passed away
I embraced the reality
Of this rivalry
And realised in essence
Who was my real family.
A tough long and hard lesson to learn
When all that was necessary
Was to release and let go
Create and maintain firm boundaries.

A new chapter beckons
As I approach the end of my 48th year
I feel that I have come home
Not back to Africa
But deep inside
To a place of knowing
That I am more than my colour
More that my hair
More than my features
More than my culture
I know the difference between religion and spirituality
I am ultimately
A child of the universe
Here to discover how to live and move freely
Full of love and compassion
In this world that I entered
And have maneuvered through each experience.
I am better able and equipped to strip away
The labels, perceived limitations and boundaries
To stand in my own truth as co-creator with my creator
Living my purpose to serve
With the gifts that have been bestowed upon me.
Utilising the power of thought with greater awareness
Knowing and feeling
Recognising it is to my strongest vibration
That the Universe will always respond.

You did nothing wrong

We enter into this world
And are shaped by primary carers.
Some stories we can tell
Others we bury inside us
The only way childhood to survive.

We push them down deep
Hoping the memories will die
And for a while
You know they do
But soon the turmoil begins,
We start to act out
Or spiral in.
Those memories may be buried
But the energy lives on
And governs many of the choices we make.

We go on
trying to piece together our lives
From the credentials
Society deems good and right.
All appears perfect on the surface
As we keep up appearances

with the Jones'
Until, one day a sudden shift.

Forgotten memories
of yesteryear
Rise up
and flash before our eyes
No more
do they want to hide
No longer
are you able to keep them down
They want to be acknowledged
Come out of the dark
and into the light.

The emotions
that was far too heavy
Deep and dark to handle
That's the child thinking
I was the one to blame
Along with guilt
these emotions
Now need putting to shame.

You need to know
You did nothing wrong
Those that should have known
Better feed you a lie
And no longer does the Universe
Want that to dampen your life.

It is resurrection time!
Dismantle the story,
separate the parts
And discover who you are.
You are not the pain
that was on you inflicted
Unveil now
The beauties of
That innocent inner child.

Shower her with love and affection
True self love
that cannot be denied
For as you acknowledge
and step into the truth
of who you are
The victim role
has no choice
but to step aside.

Take to flight

They were my dearest,
To me the closest
Thought they'd be happy
The changes to see,
Celebrate with me
All the hard work I had done
Oh so wrong.
My troubles had just begun.
For everything
I had made attempt to achieve
A web of hostility
Appeared to be spun.

I could not believe
How badly they treated
Me,
Is that how much I was really hated?
And so I withdraw,
Became totally guarded
My heart and good will
Had to be protected.

A wall of defence,
I firmly erected
Nothing through which
Could be penetrated.
The wall so high
Reinforced with self-hatred
Allowed me to hide,
I was well protected.

Protected I thought
But with handy work not perfected
Cracks in my mortar
Caught other eyes being projected
On those things about me
In words they complimented
'Leave me be!
It's not true.' I silently protested.
They spoke these words,
For of me it was something they wanted.

I was not about to give of myself,
Don't be stupid!
So they could use me, pick me apart,
And then leave me rejected?
All the pain I felt
Could not be comprehended
I had once given freely of myself,
I'd not pretended

Only to be ridiculed, the very who I was,
My heart with their lies had been impregnated

So now what grew inside suffocated
The real truth about me
That was on my soul imprinted
And as these labels
Through life became tightly pasted
I, the real I, that my Maker created.
Into the distance
That I became faded.

The awakening that I was here for a reason
And not as a target for others to poison
Allowed me the labels to begin to unfasten
And with each removal,
I felt something inside strengthen.

I am here to be without excuse or explanation
No need to fight to be heard, to be seen
I just remain open
I bathe in self-love and admiration
And I am free to be,
Totally self-accepting.

So the wounds are being healed
The walls are tumbling down
To create change
Circles and cycles must be broken

I know that now
No need to fight to be heard,
To be seen or accepted
I embrace my change and move with grace
Out of the old and into the new
I have learned how, when and why
To spread my wings and fly.

Rise

Create something new

If it appears,
That we constantly experience
the same old hurt and pain,
Then a true sense of Self
may need to be regained.
From nature and nurture
to society's demands,
Belief patterns are created
And in the subconscious mind
become ingrained.
Opportunities will be presented
again and again,
To teach forgiveness,
To release guilt, shame and blame.
Life wants for us to acknowledge
all of the self-limiting traits,
Let them go
And in their place, create
Affirmations that will initiate new growth
For what we desire, of our lives,
Is to live authentically,
Directed by the soul
Life can be lived harmoniously.

it

You notice it
It is nothing
So you forget it
Then it reappears
A few more times
It returns
You see it
Choose to ignore it
Then it shows up again
And again and again
Now you look at it
You start to wonder about it
What am I going to do with it?
Address it?
No, I'll leave it
It starts to hit
Now you feel it
It is messing with my routine
It is making me appear to be out of control
Stop it!
But it is growing
It is showing
Up everywhere

It is infiltrating other areas of my life
What is it?
Why it?
Ok it!
I am ready to listen
I am ready to see
I am ready to learn
I am ready for change
I am ready to grow
Thank you it
Look forward
To being more welcoming of it
Next time
For a smoother transit.

Dont be afraid to wake the lion

The buttons to press, you know
And I become lost in your world.
The need to please, the foe
Ever since a little girl.
Unrecognised
Coaxed me into places
I really did not want to go.
For your need was greater than mine
And all that was known was to satisfy.
To make everyone happy
Give myself away
A falsehood I had been taught
My truth mystified.
Show up and meet the basic need
To be taken care of
Use to mesmerise
And it's mistaken for true love.
Where were the examples
To stand strong in authentic power?
To say no to the coward
Who disguised the truth
For pieces of my soul to devour?
But this very experience was necessary

To create a stir and ignite the fire
It was time to stand up, get out, move forward
T'was an ever increasing desire.
Awakening to the truth
Of who I was not and who I am
What life was this that I must resist
For fear of disturbing the sleeping lion?
But as the bondage loosened
And links in the chain began to break,
Habitual behaviour began to unravel.
I stopped and often have to marvel
At the empowered choices I now make

From a cycle of confusion,
With countless coincidences
Within I developed a thirst.
For self-love
And to be trusting of
My intuition
On the list of how to be
That must always come first.

Knowledge of Self

I feel empty
Clean Empty
Real
Released from all that sabotaged and 'stealed'.
I am refreshed
Created within me is a clean heart
And a right spirit renewed
With God's Holy Spirit I have been imbued
From grace
I once fell
With my soul
It is now well
I have come home
To the truth of who I am
By clearing all that I took into my temple
That surely did not belong.
Out with self-hate
Out with self-abuse
Out with guilt
And out with shame
Out with lack
And not enough
Time to raise my game

Out with doubt
And out with fear
No longer are you welcomed here.
With self-belief, self-worth and courage
And unwavering faith
In abundance
They have been replaced
And to those dark places
I declare
This is where I stand,
There is only room for love and light here.
For I with the Creator am one.

Rise

Rise.
Stand.
It's a new day
So grand.
Past hurts and pains
Completely left behind.
You hold in your heart
love
And in your mind
Positive thoughts,
Tools
That will assist and support
Every step you now take.

Walk, knowing, who you are.
Powerful
And beautifully made.
Say thank you
Everyday
For all that you have.
Give, in full measure
Love
wherever you can.

Follow your gut feeling
It will never lead you astray.
Believe
Who they say they are
When they show you the signs,
Move in truth
And with integrity.

Set your goals,
Surrender up.
Observe the manifestations
As the Universe

Simply follow your instructions.
It's your intentions
That creates your reality.
Watch old patterns
All that no longer serve
Simply
disappear.

Rise in your truth.
Stand in your truth.
Walk in your truth.
Speak your truth.
Let no one
But you define who you are.

Rise.
Stand.
Walk.

Speak
It is new day

Opportunities lie before you
Cease then with both hands,
With each one
Do the best you can.
Joy
Happiness,
Courage
Are yours.
Spirit guides
And guardian angels
Are always near.
Connect
Through nature daily
And them you will
Always hear.

Be the best version
Of you.
Breathe
Embrace the very best.

Rise in your truth.
Stand in your truth.
Walk in your truth.
Speak your truth.
Be all that you are here to be.

Sing!

To sing
Brings
Something
That I could
Have never imagined.
Sing with heart
Sing with Soul
Sing revelations
As they unfold.
To express
Yes, blessed
There is none
Less
I am because you are
Complete, oneness
You said
I am in the father
And the father is in me
I have now come
Too understand
I too
Am Divinity
I came, take the strain

Of being on earthly plane
I'm in it, free spirit
To discover
New domain
As woman
Strong
With conviction
African
Jamaican
Briton
In- flu-ence
My thoughts, my words
My very actions
Here
On purpose
With purpose
Standing on the shoulders
Of those that came before us.
Courageous
Spontaneous
Got to be victorious
There is no option
No place for excuses.
Truths find
And mind
Don't become blind –
Dead by
The material
The superficial
Well-constructed elements
That can sabotage

The mental
The spiritual
Those parts of you
That need to flow freely
Feed
And breed
Indeed
Like rabbits
New idea
That takes shape
With action
Construction
Make it become
Habit.
So guided
Provided for
By the one that reigns above and below
In me
All about me
I flow
And show
The essence of life
When I bask in the glow.
Meditation
Raise vibration
With commitment
Invites inspiration
It is, just so
To sing
Brings
Something

That I could
Have never imagined.
Sing with heart
Sing with Soul,
Sing revelations as they unfold.

Room to flow

Almost full
To the brim.
Little space
To move in.
Becoming stagnant
No movement

The world 70% plus
Is made up of the water
Moving
Flowing
Constantly maintaining
Earth's natural law and order.

So the Creator
The wise initiator
Made us to live
In harmony.
How come we
Take much more
Than we need?
For too much greed.

Struggling to swim in
The material things
We continue to buy
Satisfying needs
That last just for a while
We create our own
Internal landfill

Ill from the stench
Of decaying superficial wants
We told ourselves
We deserve
Because we worked so hard on
Hating Monday mornings

More, more, more
Dumping
Leaving
No space
To maneuvere in
It truly is absurd
Balance must be observed
Mind body and spirit
Must flow freely
Escape rigidity
Create space
And maintain
Fluidity

The Path of the Wise

Nothing is withheld from the wise.
Those from whom
Man's construct have stepped outside.
For they know
Who holds the master key,
The One who opens the doors
Of opportunity.
They walk their path
No ladders to climb
The pursuit to rise
An illusion, pure fallacy.
With gratitude they receive
And they freely give
From the well of inner abundance
That life has blessed us all with.

Unbiased Pendulum

Karma hurry up and come.
Oh the satisfaction
to watch the table turn
On someone
Who on me
Has inflicted
Some form of atrocity.
But wait!
I stop and I reflect.
Is it now all even?
Have the scales now settled
And balanced is the sum?

Have I now reaped
consequences
For seeds that I have sown
With the inevitable resurgence
Of Karmas unbiased pendulum?

Karma you hand back to us
the full measure of our thoughts, words and actions

Karma, we can trust we will receive

in alignment with our true convictions
Be it not of love
And out of fear we choose
The hurt that breaks us
as a lesson we must use,
to guide us back to that loving place
from which deeds can naturally flow
out of good intentions.
Karma can then return to us and we are joyful
For we are showered with
what can only be
What we deserve
Countless blessings.

Price Of Love

Love changes everything

As the moth to light has an affinity,
effortlessly
you embraced your destiny.
Energies vibrating on the same frequency
Two hearts gravitate
Drawn into the sea of love,
All that you are deserving of.
Captivated,
I stand ashore,
feet sinking into the soft sand
As I marvel at the synchronicity,
My heart full of joy
for your acquaintance with absolute bliss.
Carried by the waves of seductive emotions
You rise and fall,
Higher, deeper
Taken further,
into the abyss.
Now oceans apart
Life as it was,
is rearranged
The glory days
now memories to be cherished.

Love so strong
plunge some hearts fully under.
Lovers breathe each other's air
And friendship is left adrift.

The Contract

Perplexed
I've tried
Countless times
To disregard
What's inside
You ask me why
And how could I?
These feelings
Will just not be denied
Acknowledgement
Total acceptance
In alignment
With soul's agreement
Authorised, the contract
Has been signed
And must be honoured
Preferably
in this lifetime

To the majority
Unacceptable
Indigestible
Incredible

That under such scrutiny
It was manageable
Not without guilt
And sometimes shame
But it was part of the process
To attain
And sustain
The ordained
To tear away from
The conventional
The traditional
And still remain
Sane

These scenarios
By design
Are the teachers
That provide
necessary tools
That uncover
An array of priceless treasure
That of inner strength
Courage and wisdom
We embrace our true worth
and measure
With the lessons learned
from each challenge we overcome

Now More
Power-ful

Joy Filled
I rise and soar
my earthly assignment
The next clause
I am now
ready for.

gut instinct

Yes you said.
Soon you said.
Trust me you said.
What sense is there in settling for empty words?
When gut instinct the unspoken truth has long ago heard.

Let go

My heart has felt the blows
Of love gone wrong
And I've penned the words
That writes the song
Of the muddled emotions
That seeps from its chambers
All that I've been taught about love
Has been burned to cinders.
Debris, ashes, now slowly meanders
Like sludge through my vessels
Permeating every tissue,
Every sinew, every cell.
I can hardly move
Nothing but chaos and confusion.
I am gasping for air
Desperately searching for something,
Anything that I've been told,
Like the phoenix
to rise up
And for me to still remain true.

A cascade of numbness invades.
My frazzled mind relentlessly triggers

Trying to make sense of the changes.

As day becomes night
And night becomes day
I am faced with two choices.
I can continue to allow
The feeling to poison me
Drain the life from me
Making me a shadow of who I am,
Or I can let go
Of what once was
I mean those beliefs
That are now not able to stand.
Made me make choices
That were then necessary in the process
As part of this bigger plan.
When it's time to grow,
Move to the next level
Life always presents
The necessary circumstance.
It may not be pleasant,
It may not be easy to swallow
But as we learn from each experience
We know to trust the process
Then we can,
More readily
let it go.

Love Hearts

My mind struggled to unravel
What to my spirit was already known?
Our lives together, this time
Was approaching
The final count down.

The day you told me
You were vacating
On an island in the sun,
Was the very day
I popped my first one.
Self-medication begun
13 April 2014.

While for weeks you enjoyed
The beauties of your homeland,
I soon discovered
I had developed,
For love hearts, a habit
On route
To becoming an addiction.

Long after sunset
Stars, twinkling in the night sky
Tormented, unable to rest
I took to the streets
Coat thrown over
My night dress
The 24/7, the dealer
That sold the fix
To satisfy my need .

My world revolved around you
My lover, my darling soul mate
And even after you returned
Something inside me continued to ache.
The only way to appease
this chemically driven craving
To put my mind at rest
Was to take in every gram
For instant satisfaction
Each morning now
They became
The breaker of my fast.
On your return,
The doctor confirmed
You broke the devastating news
4 March 2015.

10pm the night before,
Will I ever see you again?

To my journal I put the question
A connection so strong
Now I know can never be denied
With spirit, there are no barriers
No obstructions

You defied space and time
And in your airy presence
I found sweet comfort and belly laughter
In flesh no more to be seen
But great memories to relive
That through grieving
Comes some 3 years after
9 November 2015.

Now when I think of you,
I know the truth absolute
Albeit unconventional
My love for you and you for me
Was unconditional.

The message on each sugared tablet
I did not take the time to read,
From childhood memories
Return to me, now with ease
And I hear your spirit whisper gently to my heart
Love you,
Kiss,
Smile,
You're mine

Thinking of you,
Be happy,
goodbye.
My sunshine.

A faint echo

People come
and people go
Sometimes fast
sometimes slow
Whilst together we dance
to the melodious sounds
Intrinsic
We make sweet music
Our individual notes
come together
And we begin to move
to a new tempo
From our vibrations created
New chords orchestrated
Heart strings stroked
Oh the joy of each note
Yours in harmony with mine.
We play our tune
But sometime soon
Who struck the wrong note?
Who moved prematurely?
Jumped keys?
Painful to experience

The pace no longer rhythmic
Disrupted is the harmony
You playing your own
I'm playing mine.
Opposite ends of the scale.
People come
and people go
Sometimes fast
sometimes slow
A short sweet melody
A tune that should have ended
Stuck on repeat
A sweet, long lasting,
blissful symphony
A heavy handed collision of keys,
disaster
Music sometimes
that we just always want to remember
People come
and people go
Sometimes too fast
How could you go?
An unfinished melody
Standing in mid air
You left
And I'm holding breath
This is too long a pause
The sound of music
We played out in life together
Will it be played again,
No, never

As the years pass by
They only remain
A faint
Echo
Inside.

Soul Contract

My heart expands for I sense all about me
Your smile of admiration
of the queen I have become
The queen that you could see,
but for me was unrevealed
So much work yet to be done.

I loved you unconditionally
That, I convinced myself to believe
Meaning? I accepted less
than I truly deserved
Because it was all about
The anticipation of the attention
That quenched
the longing for you feeling.
You snatched my breath away.

Thought it was love
And yes it was
But what kind of love
shrouds the heart
And causes the soul to diminish?
For all you live for

is to please
Meeting others wants and wishes.

Unconsciously, through no fault of their own
Raised, I was to put people first
Sacrifice
To attain love
That was the strongest message
And become my personal curse.

That's what I was shown
And although physically grown
My emotional mind was still infantile
Longing for
Seeking for
Craving for
Daddy's approval and love
The substitute became
What we had.

I could not bear the thought
That you were about to leave
I would no longer be able to take and hold that long breathe
No more would I be able
To bury my head
Into your chest
And oh how my heart grieved.

But sometimes, I get this feeling
From the deepest depths of me, a knowing

That you made a sacrifice
That you chose to leave
So that I could have the chance to breathe
To inhale
And finally exhale
And to continue breathing
A second chance
To release
To heal, reveal and embrace
My status as Royalty
To be the queen
That even from your wounded heart
Totally unknown to me
You could clearly see.

Soul contracts honoured
Each one's purpose fulfilled.

Fresh Start

Some things
sometimes
are best left unsaid
The drama
has been acted
The book
already read
So what more
do you think
there is left to say
Go on guilty conscience
Please go away

Find some other way
to play your game
By doing a replay
there is nothing to gain
Is that what you live for?
Torment and torture
I am having joyful times
I have discovered true laughter

Go on

go away
just leave me be
I've found a new way
to do life,
I feel so free
So don't you try come
to weigh me down
With mistakes
from my past life
Do you hear how you sound?
I am here
and have no more price to pay
I have forgiven myself
Allow me
to be on my way
Water under the bridge
And off a duck's back
Over my head
You know you just have to stop!

Joyful Tears

I cry not because I am sad
I cry because I am glad
I am so full of praise and gratitude
For the life I now have.

Once all was murky, so unclear
Did not know why I was here.
Tossed and blown with every wind
Seeking at every stop
To find some meaning
Finding none.
Then whipped up and tossed again and again.
This way and that way
His way and her way
Up and down
Round and around and around
And going – no where!

Had to develop roots
Took time
But now I know the truth

Today I have meaning

Today I have purpose
To live and inspire
Is my service
With my soul as director
I am the wiser
I know who I am
I see, I hear, I feel, I taste, I smell
The joys of life
In whatever form they take
I am rooted and grounded
By universe supported
I am connected

Now do you understand?
I cry not because I am sad
I cry because I am glad
I am filled and overflowing with gratitude and praise
For the life I now have.

An Angel came into my life

An angel came into my life
And encompassed me.
Beams of light penetrated and illuminated my whole being
And me became acquainted with I
A part me
Little I barely knew,
Forgotten attributes
That doctrinarian did it's best to diminish
Obliterate into non-existence.

An Angel came into my life
And as he lovingly, kindly, gently
Made himself known to me,
I felt a fountain of peace, of happiness, of joy
Refreshingly spring from within me,
Restoring the respect, honour and power
Of a Goddess that had been overthrown by negativity

An angel came into my life
Teaching me to accept the good and not so good
That personifies who I am
I was strongly advised
That attempting to change just to please,

There was absolutely no need.
I was reminded just to give thanks
For the gift of life I take in each breathe,
To embrace opportunities on my life's journey
That presents themselves and dig deep to overcome each of
my tests.

An Angel came into my life
And inspired a new way of being
Living in the moment,
Taking it only for what it is
Nothing more, nothing less
Not demanding, not resisting,
Not digging in heels to have that which cannot be 'haved'.

An angel came into my life
A truly beautiful, restorative experience
Now etched in the memory of my body's every cell
And now when life becomes cumbersome
And I need a place to rest
The Angel taught me how to return to that place,
The source of my happiness.

An Angel came into my life
Revealing wonderful truths,
I am so grateful to be left with
An angel came into my life
And I now I know again
What it means to live.

Lightworker

He was black and comely
Glowing intensely
He stepped in
And like a ray of sunshine
His presence fell upon me
His beam
Dispelled my confusion
In return
Her radiance and sparkle
Illuminated a trace of uncertainty
And to him offered
Sweet clarity
Lightworkers encounters
Sheds light
Insight
For the next right step of the journey.

No Coincidence

This day
This way
This time
Notice
All the signs.
The Unseen at working in our favour
Utilising Divine Law and Order
Personality with purpose to align.

The trappings of this physical material world
Become the shepherd that lead some like sheep astray
Like lambs to the slaughter
Uniqueness is betrayed.
Break away seek to reveal the spark, no the light
That within resides
Use to decipher
And reveal the codes that come to guide

You
To live a life of freedom
Come out from among them
No longer be swayed by them
And become an unconscious victim

Fooled into thinking
That you have everything
There is so much more to living
Than the superficial havings
That masks the deep meaning of life.

A butterfly catches your eye
A song plays in the distance, you recognise
A word pops into your head, why?
Someone you've not seen
Shows up after such a long time
You realise
These coincidences form the arrow
That from the norm points to brighter skies
Now courage is all you need
To do that which you have already considered
But was just too afraid to try.

Life is for
living

Universe Has My Back

Come rain or shine
I am now always
happily on time
A far cry away
From the days
When with a passion
I loathed every Monday
And like one lost in the dessert longs for rain.
I craved for the joy
Of embracing Fridays.
Each week day morn
I swallowed the bitter pill
That raised the mask
And induced the will
To keep on going
Just to pay the bills.

Feel the fear and do it anyway
Finally decided to walk the talk
Stopped pretending
Gave up trying
To make it all work
Surrendered to my soul's call

To the thud in my gut
And trusted that
Universe always has my back
From sunrise to sun set
Life is more the sweeter
I experience all the greatness
I am made of
Wealth in abundance, unmeasured
Wealth not defined
Merely by figures.

Doors open
Doors close
I hold on to nothing
I go with the flow
Giving thanks for every miracle
Every blessing
Which I can see
More clearly now
Received from my Creator
Who guides me
Instructs me how
To lift up my head
And keep my feet firmly on the ground.

The Promise

Colours arched across the sky,
The spectrum
gracefully suspended
Cannot be denied.
Heart-warming,
Breath-taking,
of a great promise,
it is a sign.
Lest I forget,
I am reminded,
Always to remember
As above, so it is below.
As I rest my eyes upon
The prism effect
Of the rain meets the sun.
It causes the corners of my mouth to rise
And it softens my brow.

All is well, I am assured
No matter what the situation
No matter what the time.
The priceless treasures of life itself
Peace joy happiness love

The very essence of my being,
So sublime.

Resonate, radiates
Is magnified
By messages from nature
So awesome in design.

Up in a tree

Peace
Tranquillity
My inner being
Content
I gaze upwards
Shades of green form a canopy
That gracefully sway
When caressed by the gentle breeze
As it passes through.

Fully supported
Fully protected
Birds conversing happily.
Do you have a message for me?
So used to the humming sound of the traffic in the distance
That's part and parcel of nature in the city.
I observe joggers passing
Panting heavily,
I remember that is meant to be me
But today
I decided
Just to be
And found myself
Up in a tree.

Siberian Warrior

Checks at the crack of dawn
Breakfast?
Costume?
Makeup?
What a transformation
Now we are being jetted off
To a secret location

A quarry
In the Welsh valleys
Blue skies and
Blazing sun
Inhale
Exhale
Wow, this is
So breath-taking

Poised on a flat rock
The moment
Fully embracing
Soon I'm off
Floating

Startled back into reality
By the Assistant Director's first call
Immediately recanted
We can relax
Today I am happy with that
As I settle back down on my bed of rock

What?
Lunch?
Already?
Such an easy morning
Now it's time for action
Armed and charging into battle
Perfectly captured in one take
The Director couldn't be happier
Now for the main role
I have been hired for today
Dead Siberian warrior

No care for a feature
Or a walk on role
Just happy am I
To lie down
Awoken by the jubilant words
'That's a wrap!'
I cannot believe it,
It's already 6 O'clock.

The perfect Monday
Back on the job

I was able to lie down and completely recover
From a weekend of indulgence
That had left me
With a Monday morning hangover.

Culture

Me nuh wha guh a inglan!

Run weh guh a bush
Run guh hide
whe dem cya fine yuh
Run hard
an nuh look back
Me nuh wha guh ah Inglan
De madda country
whe de people and the wedda
come like one
Dem harsh likka wah.
Me and dem nah gree
Pick up yuh foot and run
De street coulda pave
wid gol likle more
Me ah stay inna me island
me nuh ceer
if me stay yah an poor.

Me, full up ah talent
Me cya read
and write
and duh me sums
Ah inna baby class

dem ah guh put me
Tell me seh
Me cya
pronounce me word propa
So dem
haffi class me as dunce

Left me mek me stay
wid mamma and papa
Ah dem me know
as ma and pa
Me nuh wha hear
bout no new bradda or sista
Dem ah guh wah treat me
like me ah out cyass
Me nuh wah live weh
When yuh blow bret
yuh bret freeze
as it lef yuh mout
Ar whe me hav fi waak
in a trees and fours
Just fi safely get bout

Dem people dem nuh freid
fi come tek set pan yuh,
Just because yuh black
Dem gittup every day
And circulate
like wile daag
Bout we box food

out ta dem mout
So ah we
de mwah fi attack

It nuh matta
wedda dem a civilian ar official
We nuh duh dem a ting
When dem ready
dem tek dem chain and batn
Ah pure lick
pan we de mwah fling

Lef me mek me stay ah me yaad,
Country life ah seh one fi me
Me hun waan guh lack up
in na nuh brick house
Unno did tink a factory
True unno did see smoke
a come out a de chimney.

Muummy and daddy,
unnu gwaan guh spen
unnu likle five years
When unu ready fi come back,
Me wi still deh yah
Me nuh wha guh an inglan
Cause whe me check it out
Laax
Nuh weh
Nuh betta
Dan yaad!

Invisible

Natural daylight
Does my dark hue
Not make me
The more visible?
Patiently I wait
In this queue
And find it quite remarkable.
You force your eyes
To seek out
Diluted shades behind.
Next please, you call
Thanks for waiting
This really is unbelievable.

Inside your mind what goes on
That concur by the majority
Such unjust behaviour?
Have you been fitted with
An automatic switch
When dark tones present
Please ignore is what you register?
Do you seek to initiate
The age old lie that you have been fed

To reinforce?
The I told you so
Their heart is dark, full of anger
Just too emotional.

I respond and your belief system
Is blown right out of the water.
How uncomfortable you now look and sound
In your futile attempts to cover over
Your ingrained and blatant detest of me
With superficial laughter -
And the one that stood behind
That stepped up in front
Like you, really is no better.
In unison, the programmed response
Both apologise
Didn't see you.
Oh so sorry.
A different time
A different place
Yet the same old answer!

Roots Music

Sounds so familiar
Even though
I've never heard it before
Somehow it is recognisable
and moves me at my core.
Can that be?
Not a groove of which I know
from my love of soul music
It is a riddim
That takes over
my whole body system.
A holistic vibe
De beat somehow
tells me
I belong
to a long lost tribe?
The drum beat, my heart beat
The base line, my waist whine
Beat de drum, my whole body hum
Hit the base,
I can hear, I can feel, I can taste
Africa
Africa

Africa
The lyrics speak the truth
Of where I come from
Gives me back
my rich history
Way before
The struggle
That came
with colonisation.
There's a natural mystic
flowing in the air
We de pan a level vibes
A higher frequency
The chains of oppression
Fall from my heart
and from my mind.
We jump and skank and we rock
We feel a sense of liberty
Not the false liberty,
beaten into my fore parents
and used as a weapon
to uphold slavery
Telling me that Jesus save
And our masters we must obey.
When I hear dis music
My soul is set free
Ah new kind of live - ity
The drum beat, my heart beat
The base line, my waist whine
Beat de drum, my whole body hum
Hit the base,

I can hear, I can feel, I can taste
Africa
Africa
Africa
The land my ancestors come from.
Africa is alive in me
Especially
when I hear
the sound
of
the drum.

Emotional Baggage

When? Where? Why?
How did you manage to accumulate so much?
Yuh ah nuh garbage truck.
Who said that? Is that fact?
Oh my! What a load you carry pan you back.

He said.
She said.
They said.
You take up all the negative energy.
Now, you angry, annoyed, disappointment,
You feel a void
Embarrassed, guilty, judged, destroyed.

Baggage. Emotional baggage.
When unprocessed,
Left to festa
Yuh know seh only more and more is attracted.
Release the emotional baggage
off you back,
off you shoulda
off you waist
off you belly,

off you hip
off you leg
An off you finga.

From you kidney, yuh liva,
your pancreas, gallbladda,
From you lungs
And from your heart
Ah dem place guilt and shame,
Sadness and grief go an sekle
Den solidify
and dependant on who you are,
Restrict different body parts.

Emotional baggage
Time to unload, off load!
Free up youself man
Find strent in you back bone
And 'tand up strong.
Allow no one to knock you confidence.

Like the mini bus conducta in Jamaica
seh 'Let aaf driva'
Ah soh you must drop off
All weh nuh belongs
Pan you shoulda!

Rock the Boat

I ain't rocking the boat
I gots to stay afloat
Ain't no capsizing going on here.
What you talking about?
I have no fear
I just want things to be calm
No need to be creating any alarm
Just plain sailing
That's all I'm saying
In that, where is the harm?

What's wrong with things staying
Just the way they've always been?
Change, what for? Nothing here broken
That I've seen.
Why you want to come
With all this
New finding, new thinking
Why you tripping?
Just do what we've always done
It's been working from the beginning.
All this talk of hearts and minds expanding

I am real happy in my little comfort zone
Where all things are familiar
Aren't you safe within your boarders?
Doing what you been taught you ought ah?
So now you want to open your mouth and speak out
You want to take action, draw attention
Something you been ok with
Now you ain't feeling good about?
Why can't you just toe the line
And keep yourself out of trouble?
I hear you! I hear you!
But now is not the time
This is crazy talking
come on quit
Out of here on the double!

But as I choose to take a look around me
With eyes of awareness wide open
I see for real what you say is going on.
Why do I now feel broken?
In solidarity let me now join you
In tipping this boat over
Stretch ourselves and swim
To fulfil our mission
Even if it means
That sometimes we may be taken under.
Just take a breath
Hold it long enough, release
And trust in the Higher Power
We are not here to play it safe
In its fullness, life we must taste

Trust the convictions as they come
And in our authentic self
Know and feel we belong
Never be afraid to do what must be done
'cos if we don't
It'll keep hitting us
Upside the head!

Choices decisions

Choices, decisions
we've all got to make them
Choices decisions
that's what makes life happen
Choices decisions
big ones small ones
Choices decisions
rushed ones
those deliberated on
Choices decisions
affect you affect me
To a greater or lesser degree
What is my contribution
Will my choices my decisions be lessons or blessings
From the Law there is no escaping
What we put out
will surely be returning
Bible echoes universal Law
The seeds that are sown
is what we will be reaping
Individual choices individual decisions
To universal consciousness
makes a contribution

So what we emit,
What is our strongest collective vibration
Will result, all around us,
in its manifestation
Self-awareness is the key
So when i look in the mirror
let my reflection be
Evidence of my choices and decisions
Those attributes and moral qualities
That which in the world
I wish to see.

About the Author

Vanessa has been a retail assistant, Secretary, After School Play Leader and Community Centre Assistant. She has fulfilled roles within her community as a radio presenter and as the lady with ideas and inspiration. She was born in 1967 and aged 11 years, converted to Christianity, the religion of her Jamaican born parents, who settled in England in 1962.

She embarked on a career path to become a Biology Teacher in 1999. In her final year of her Applied Biological Sciences degree, ill health brought her studies to a halt. She was forced to be still. In these soul searching months, she discovered her choices had been influenced by external pressures and expectations, She began to ask the bigger questions of life, 'Who am I? Why am I here? What is my purpose?' These questions took her on a journey of self-discovery after she read her first book on spirituality, 'Tapping the Power Within' by Iyanla Vanzant.

The study of alternative approaches to life in particular naturopathy and holistic therapies redirected her focus and supported a transformation. She went on to qualify with diplomas to become a Holistic Therapist and Natural Nutrition Practitioner. Vanessa set up her practice in 2010 and facilitated the healing of her clients for 7 years.

She took the courageous step of terminating her most recent role in retail to finally commit to fulfill her childhood desire and to use her natural talents as a creative. Vanessa is a singer, songwriter, supporting actor and creator of GUCO natural skincare.

In March 2018, Vanessa began to write spontaneously on a daily basis for a period of two weeks. On completion, she discovered she had written her life experiences and insights in rhyme. The collection of prose and poems has become her first book, Rise to Freedom, Her story in Rhyme.

9 781982 218669